WHAT DOES A FIREFIGHTER DO?

What Does a Community Helper Do?

Erin Schmidt

Words to Know

bunker coat (BUHN-kur koht)—Heavy coat worn to protect firefighters from heat.

bunker pants (BUHN-kur pants)—Heavy pants worn to protect firefighters from heat.

community (ku-MYOO-ni-tee)—A group of people who live in the same area.

dispatcher (dis-PA-chur)—A person who answers a 911 call and tells firefighters where to go.

pumper truck (PUM-pur truk)—Truck that pumps water through fire hoses.

siren (SIGH-run)—Loud alarm on a fire truck that tells other drivers to move out of the way.

sledgehammer (SLEDJ-ha-mur)—Large, heavy hammer used to punch through walls and knock open doors.

Enslow Elementary
an imprint of

E Enslow Publishers, Inc.
40 Industrial Road
Box 398
Berkeley Heights, NJ 07922
USA

PO Box 38
Aldershot
Hants GU12 6BP
UK

http://www.enslow.com

Contents

Some firefighters sleep at the fire station. They always have to be ready.

Fire!

Rrrring! Rrrring!
The alarm goes off at the fire station. The firefighters get out of bed. The dispatcher talks over the radio. She tells the firefighters that a house is burning.

Firefighters have to know how to drive fire trucks.

Firefighters on the Way

The firefighters rush to the fire trucks. The captain makes sure all the firefighters are ready to go. The driver turns on the flashing lights and sirens. He honks the horn to warn other drivers: "Move out of the way!"

coat

helmet

pants

boots

Firefighters wear helmets, boots, coats, and pants to protect them from getting hurt.

What Do Firefighters Wear?

Firefighters put on special clothes to keep them safe. Helmets and hoods protect the firefighters' heads. Boots protect their feet. Bunker coats and bunker pants keep the firefighters from getting burned.

Firefighters rescue people using long ladders.

What Do Firefighters Do?

The firefighters arrive at the scene. They check to make sure no people are in danger. They rescue people who are trapped. Firefighters help people who are hurt.

Every firefighter has a special job to do.

The fire chief gives each firefighter a job. One firefighter runs the pumper truck while another sprays water. Other firefighters climb ladders. Firefighters must work together to put out the fire.

axe

sledgehammer

fire hydrant wrench

fire hydran

Firefighters use special tools.

What Do Firefighters Use?

Firefighters use special tools. An axe is used to chop holes. A sledgehammer is used to break open doors. A wrench is used to open fire hydrants.

Firefighters keep working even after the fire has been put out. They need to find out what caused the fire.

The Fire Is Out

After the fire is out, the firefighters keep working. They spray more water to make sure the fire does not start again. They search to find why the fire started. Firefighters even help people find a new place to stay for the night.

Firefighters keep their trucks clean and shiny.

Firefighters clean their tools, trucks, and clothes after a fire. They wash and load the hoses. They fill the fire truck tanks with water.

After a hard day's work, the firefighters go to sleep until the next alarm rings.

Firefighters Are Heroes

When their work is done, the firefighters go back to the fire station. There they wait for the next fire alarm. Firefighters must always be ready to help. Firefighters are community heroes.

Home Escape Plan

Ask the adults you live with to help you make a home escape plan.

First, draw a map of your home. Draw lines to show two different ways to get out of your bedroom. In a real fire, you might need to leave your home through a window. Never go outside through your window unless it is an emergency.

Next, choose a safe place outside where you and your family can meet. Write the name of that place on your map. Post your escape plan on a bulletin board, wall, or refrigerator. Finally, hold a family fire drill to practice your escape plan.

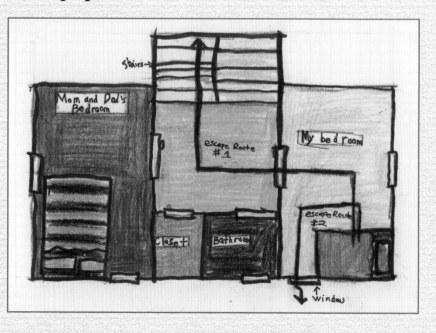

Learn More

Books

Adamson, Heather. *A Day in the Life of a Firefighter.* Mankato, Minn.: Capstone Press, 2004.

Schaefer, Lola. *Who Works Here: Fire Station.* Chicago, Illinois: Heinemann Library, 2001.

Internet Addresses

The Great Sparky the Fire Dog
<http://www.nfpa.org/sparky/>
  Learn about fire safety.

Welcome to the USFA's Kids Page: Where the Fun Starts
<http://www.usfa.fema.gov/kids>
  Learn how you can be safe.

Index

Note to Teachers and Parents: The *What Does a Community Helper Do?* series supports curriculum standards for K–4 learning about community services and helpers. The Words to Know section introduces subject-specific vocabulary. Early readers may require help with these new words.

Series Literacy Consultant:
Allan A. De Fina, Ph.D.
Past President of the New Jersey Reading Association
Professor, Department of Literacy Education
New Jersey City University

Enslow Elementary, an imprint of Enslow Publishers, Inc.

Enslow Elementary® is a registered trademark
of Enslow Publishers, Inc.

Copyright © 2005 by Enslow Publishers, Inc.

Library of Congress Cataloging-in-Publication Data

Schmidt, Erin.
   What does a firefighter do? / Erin Schmidt.
      p. cm. — (What does a community helper do?)
   Includes bibliographical references and index.
   ISBN 0-7660-2539-X
   1. Fire extinction—Juvenile literature. 2. Fire fighters—Juvenile literature. I. Title. II. Series.
   TH9148.S35   2005
   628.9'2—dc22   2004006892

Printed in the United States of America

10 9 8 7 6 5 4 3 2 1

To Our Readers:
We have done our best to make sure all Internet Addresses in this book were active and appropriate when we went to press. However, the author and the publisher have no control over and assume no liability for the material available on those Internet sites or on other Web sites they may link to. Any comments or suggestions can be sent by e-mail to comments@enslow.com or to the address on the back cover.

Illustration Credits: Comstock Images/Getty Images, p. 8 (center); © Royalty-Free/CORBIS, p. 16; Creatas, p. 1; Adam Crowley/PhotoDisc/Getty Images, p. 6; Hemera Technologies, Inc. 1997-2000, pp. 8 (objects around center photograph), 13, 14 (all), 19; Mark C. Ide, pp. 4, 18, 20 (bottom); Skip Nall/PhotoDisc/Getty Images, p. 12; Leslie O'Shaushnessy/Visuals Unlimited, p. 10; Thinkstock/Getty Images, p. 20 (top).

Cover Illustration: Creatas (bottom); top left to right (Skip Nall/PhotoDisc/Getty Images, p. 12; Corel Corporation; Mark C. Ide; Leslie O'Shaushnessy/Visuals Unlimited.)